D1401309

A GUIDE
TO
WATER
GARDENING

William Rae-Smith

BRACKEN BOOKS

A GUIDE TO WATER GARDENING
is published 1989 by Bracken Books
an imprint of Bestseller Publications Ltd.,
Princess House, 50 Eastcastle Street,
London W1N 7AP, England.

ISBN 1 85170 290 3

A Guide to Water Gardening
was conceived, edited, designed and
produced for Bracken Books Ltd. by
Morgan Samuel Editions
4 Somerset Road, London W13 9PB.

Editorial: Emma Worth, Paul Graham
Design: Tony Paine, Sarah Macdonald
Illustrations: Jim Robins
Picture research: Jane Lewis
Publisher: Nigel Perryman

Typeset in 10/13pt and 9/12pt Quorum by Highbridge Printing, London
Separations by Scantrans, Singapore
Printed and bound by Slovart, Czechoslovakia

The material comprising this book was
originally published as part of
THE COMPLETE BOOK OF WATER GARDENING
by BRACKEN BOOKS, 1989

CONTENTS

4

INTRODUCTION: An Inspiration and Life Force *4*; Roots in Water *4*; Religion and Symbolism *5*; Water in the Garden 6.

8
SECTION ONE – **THE PRINCIPLES OF WATER GARDENING**

STILL WATER: Animation – Europe *10*, Languid Stourhead *12*, Animating Your Pool *14*; Containment – Islamic Restraint *16*, Space and Serenity *18*, Precise Lines, Raised Pools and Borders *18*; Reflections – Reflections on Your Pool *20* ∗ MOVING WATER: Cascades and Waterfalls – The Natural Waterfall *24*; Fountains – Fountains as Symbols and in Religion *28*; The Fountain as Art *30*.

32
SECTION TWO – **WATER GARDEN TECHNIQUES**

Formal or informal *34*; Planting and Protection *35*; What kind of pool? *36*; Shape *37*; Depth *38*; Pool Liners and Pre-formed Pools 39; Installation *40*; Edging and Paving *42*; Building a Bog Garden *44*; Fountains *46*; Waterfalls *48*; *Tsukubai 50*; What Type of Water Feature? *52*; Lighting *54*; Fish *55*; Planting and Maintenance *56*; Plant Listings *58*.

62-64
INDEX and ACKNOWLEDGEMENTS

INTRODUCTION

AN INSPIRATION AND LIFE-FORCE

Many years ago, the arid heat of the desert breathed life into the sophisticated water gardens of Islam. Water became the inspiration of Islamic art, which reflected a deep appreciation for its purity and its life-giving properties. This appreciation is rarely evident today, when daily contact with water usually involves a mundane household chore. In modern industrial society the great rivers and oceans of our world are often taken for granted, abused and polluted. But the art of water gardening is inseparable from the historical uses and applications of water, and from the philosophical and spiritual systems that have grown up around water since the dawning of civilization: each element has made its contribution to the changing synthesis that lies behind the use of water for our relaxation and pleasure.

ROOTS IN WATER

The boundless desert sands appear to be beyond life, growth, time or sound. The searing wind sculpts a sinister parody of pastoral tranquillity among the dunes, with mock carvings of lakes and streams, hills and valleys, and even leisurely paths and graceful bridges. But without water, this enormous sculpture can never be more than a huge restless body of dust, encompassing over a fifth of the world's desert.

With water, however, everything has meaning. The dust of decay can be moulded to form the bricks of civilization; likewise, living cells can grow and reproduce. So water is the source of life, altering landscapes and shaping peoples. Without food, life can be sustained for months, but without water, for only days. In fact, each of us starts our life surrounded by water; for months, babies in the womb are aware of the gentle, soothing ebb and flow of the fluid in which they swim.

Our roots in water are not just physiological, though, for water is essential for every aspect of human evolution. Each great culture started its development next to a great river: Chinese civilization evolved along the banks of the *Yellow River;* the Ancient Egyptians spread outward from the *Nile*; the Indians from the *Indus* and the Persians from the *Tigris* and *Euphrates*. The flow of a river, suggesting a spring and a bourn, a beginning and an end, must have acted as a chronometer and an inspiration, a testimony to the passing of time.

Ancient man soon learnt that his development was determined by his capacity to organize and manipulate water. His first step was to develop a means of irrigating the rich alluvial plains beside rivers, thereby guaranteeing and increasing the harvest; he also quickly learnt how to use water for transport and defence.

One of the most interesting methods of primitive irrigation was the Qanat. By excavating a tunnel from a village to the subterranean water level at the base of the mountain, the ingenious ancient Persians tapped fresh water and brought it to the arid plateau where it was needed. From the air, one can see today the crater-like holes that ventilated the tunnels dug from the foot of a mountain to a distant village.

RELIGION AND SYMBOLISM

As a natural consequence to its importance to early societies, water came to play an integral part in religion and its rituals. It features frequently in the familiar Bible stories: The Great Flood that washed away evil, for example; Moses parting the Red Sea; the rite of Baptism; Jesus walking on water; the transformation of water into wine. This ritual use of water is not confined to Judaism and Christianity, but is a feature of many other religions — Hindus, for instance, practise ritual bathing before religious ceremonies.

In some theologies, though, purification through water was also associated with death. To the Romans, the River *Styx* symbolized the barrier between life and death. A coin was placed in the mouth of the dead as payment for the boatman Charon, who shipped them across the river to the underworld — a journey into the unknown. Viking dead were laid out on lavishly decorated ships to sail on a mystical voyage across the oceans to seek out a holy destination; after his death, King Arthur was placed on a barge by Sir Bedivere and escorted across the water by mysterious fair ladies to the magical Island of Avalon.

Water is often considered a feminine quality, associated with fertility. This is especially true in the Oriental concept of Yin and Yang. The former represents the soft, yielding nature of water — the common portrayal of femininity; and the latter signifies the hard and uncompromising, associated with mountains and masculinity. These categories are also apparent in

Greek mythology, in beautiful water nymphs who dote on their handsome heroes and in the masculine portrayal of Neptune, who rules over them, armed with a trident.

The Greeks believed that each stream was the home of a water spirit, so crossing water was a serious business. A bridge was considered a violation of the spirit's domain, and archaeology has revealed how women and children were buried in their foundations in order to appease the spirits. Adapted to a different civilization, the same belief has persisted to modern times: in folklore, witches are unable to cross running water and cannot pursue a victim beyond the water's edge.

Over the ages, each of the many spiritual associations has taken its place as a stone in the ever-changing mosaic of the symbolism of water. It is almost a cliche of poetry that water is the "mirror to the soul". But like all cliches, it contains an element of the truth. Perhaps this is why different people — and different peoples - see so many confused and contradictory images in water: birth or death; joy or sorrow; loss and fulfilment — which one depends on time, place, mood and tradition. To generalize, though, there are five elements in the symbolism of water: baptism and the giving of life, purification and death, the idea of a voyage and the unknown, femininity and fertility and, finally, truth.

WATER IN THE GARDEN

Because the symbolism, the properties and the associations of water are so deeply rooted in the sub-conscious, there is a mysterious comfort to be obtained from the presence of water in daily life — and, practically, that means in the garden. Its presence, brings out a primitive creativity in us, an endless curiosity. Part of the fascination may lie in water's unlimited potential to surprise and delight, because depending on its volume, its temperature and its form, water offers a myriad of different possibilities that stimulate both mind and senses. Even in the simplest of forms, such as a tub-pond or a Japanese *tsukubai*, water will bring a feeling of life and significance into even the most barren of spots. And, of course, it will attract animal life: dragonflies, birds, fish and frogs.

From the aesthetic viewpoint, water is a diverse and fascinating medium for artistic expression, and one that has been manipulated in a variety of ways throughout the history of garden design. The designer can exploit its properties of reflection and sound, its calming influence and its purity. Alternatively, the water garden can be the home of exotic plants, or a liquid extension of the architecture of the house.

On a more intimate level, a simple pond can be a self-contained microcosm of existence, where the horticulturalist can cultivate an enormous range of plants to perfect his garden; the dreamer can become absorbed in thought, lulled by the silken rustle of running water that blocks out the intrusive sound of the outside world and heightens the sense of peace and privacy within. But once more, we must return, of necessity, to the indefinable qualities of water. For it is these that make a water garden so strangely attractive, offering, even within the restricted area of a small town garden, the possibility of escape from the hubbub of modern life, and a sequestered spot in which to relax.

To be truly inspiring, though, a water garden must be designed with respect and understanding. Each garden tradition has a concept of the particular form water should take, depending to a great extent on the environment. However, cultural and horticultural traditions have often borrowed from each other, and today we have many types of water garden from which to choose. All these different traditions have had to address the same principles that govern the use of water in a garden: animation, containment, reflection and movement.

THE PRINCIPLES OF WATER GARDENING

STILL WATER
Animation — Europe, Languid Stourhead, Animating
Your Pool; Containment — Islamic Restraint, Space and
Serenity, Precise Lines, Raised Pools and Borders;
Reflections — Reflections on Your Pool.

MOVING WATER
Cascades and Waterfalls — The Natural Waterfall;
Fountains — Fountains as Symbols and in Religion;
The Fountain as Art.

The canal at Westbury Court, near Gloucester, still
reflects light at dusk, forming a mysterious visual
link with the horizon.

STILL WATER

ANIMATION

The Islamic tradition of garden design give us a fine example of how the many properties of water can be used to enhance contemplative and sensual pleasure. The water performs all kinds of technical feats, appearing in copious jets and hesitant drips, in running channels and sparkling crystalline waterfalls. But in spite of the movement in water, one always senses its languidness and peacefulness. The secret of Islamic water design lies in the simultaneous representation of stillness and movement. Water design depends on a careful juxtaposition of both these aspects, so that they complement, rather than detract from each other. Without this enhancement, neither the spirit of water, nor indeed the spirit of the viewer, can be successfully animated. This sense of animation is fundamental to every design feature.

The Islamic climate is not always the best setting for still water, as the heat can make it seem stagnant and lifeless. The pool in the Court of Myrtles in the Alhambra, in Spain, escapes this fate, however. The large expanse of water is set off by two small fountains, and a delicate stream of water, emanating from a long tongue, serves to juxtapose the contrasting qualities of water, creating ripples on the surface of an otherwise motionless pool. This subtle technique, preserving an overall effect of stillness, while at the same time animating the water, exemplifies a combination of confidence and sensitive understanding that is essential for good water design.

The great basins of water, used in the ritual performance of religious ablutions, also demonstrate an interesting visual phenomenon. The surface of the water is quite still, but because the basin is brim-full it seems constantly on the brink of overflowing.

EUROPE

In 17th-century Europe, Andre le Nôtre designed the immense and awe-inspiring water gardens at Versailles and Vaux le Vicomte. A pageant of

A poignant sculpture, by David Wynne, lends a
graceful poetry to this still pond at Easton Grey
House.

fountains jubilantly interspersing large still sheets of water is as impressive as the grand buildings themselves. At Versailles, the *parterres d'eau* were heralded as a new innovative phase in the use of water - a strong contrast with frothing fountains, they highlighted instead the possibilities of passive water in garden design. In time they came to be seen as an inspirational adaptation of water to the northern climate.

The most significant thing about these rectangular pools was their formal containment in an open setting. Unlike previous examples, such as the Court of Myrtles where the pool is enclosed by architecture, the *parterres d'eau* were completely open to natural light, reflecting the changing sky instead of buildings. Within the formal frame of the pool, the surface became a theatre of dramatic forces, of billowing clouds and piercing streaks of sunlight. The reflective properties of water here take on a cosmic scale, bringing the sky to earth and the earth to sky. This was surely the conscious desire of Louis XIV, the Sun King, whose pride and aspiration to become one with the heavens brings to mind Icarus, flying heavenwards on wings of wax.

In 18th-century England, passive water was used in a very different way in the naturalistic garden. The French garden style found little support in this moody land of fluid contour and low cloud, and instead of adopting this new taste in formal gardens the English evolved their own informal style. Rather than containing water in a formal frame, the English modelled the water feature on natural shape. The water was placed at the lowest point of the landform cradled by gentle slopes, whereas at Versailles it was raised up in basins. Used in this way it reflected not only the moods of the sky but the silhouettes of hills and the rich colours of seasonal change.

LANGUID STOURHEAD

Nowhere can the English style be seen better than at Stourhead, where the blazing reflections of autumnal leaves and of flowering rhododendrons attract admiring crowds. In the English landscape style, water gave form a context. The irregular shape and contour, the ungeometric pattern of trees, shrubs and hills in the landscape garden were given a sense of scale and unity. This idea is not unique to informal garden design, though, for the Islamic runnel and French canal used water to link separate areas of the garden. But the fact that still water lies horizontally, serves to link a variety of features in the garden cohesively and most importantly gives the scale to the overall image.

The relationship can easily be seen at Stourhead, where the water harmonizes the tall evergreen and deciduous trees with the classical

A light mist seeps over the tranquil waters of
Faringdon House, in Berkshire.

buildings, which appear with ivory opalescence against the dark dense background of trees and shrubs. A feeling of movement is achieved through reflection and through the winding contours and carefully hidden boundaries of the bodies of water. Instead of a lake, the water was made to look like an imperceptibly slow-moving and broad river, evoking a mysterious languidness that was not apparent in previous water design. This languid movement is a great part of the beauty of water cities, such as Venice, Amsterdam or Suzhou in China.

ANIMATING YOUR POOL

A sense of movement can be created in various different ways. Breezes, of course, will distort the reflections and paint a mosaic of fragmented shards of colour. In England, though, planting has always been important in design and, carefully done, this will give a sense of movement to the water feature. Even a small round pool with clearly-defined borders can be animated with plants. On hazy summer afternoons, you can savour the rich growth of the waxy lily-buds, the spreading of the leaves on the water, and listen to the whispering heads of the luxuriant marginal plants. The evenings will bring out a different beauty, as insects hover over the water and the surface prickles with activity. Aquatic life will add interest to the pool, and you can spend hours watching the flickering embers of the fish dreamily voyaging through their submarine world.

In this way, either an impression of movement, or movement itself, should be carefully considered when designing your pool. Whether formal or informal, a still water feature should express this potential for movement. After all, in its natural environment, water is in a state of flux. Small fountains and water falls, brimming water, reflection, evocative contour or planting will all contribute towards animating still water.

CONTAINMENT

The method of containment is more important in the design of passive water than in active water. Containment defines the role of the water feature. In Islamic and French gardens, water is contained within a simple formal border, which differs from the naturalistic sloping waterside of the English tradition. Each approach presents water in a different way. In mediaeval and renaissance fountains, for example, the containment was considered more important than the water itself. Water filled elaborately curved basins and spouted out of the mouths of Gothic lions, gargoyles and classical motifs. In these cases the sculptural qualities of the water have

Seemingly forgotten, mosses, ferns and moisture-
loving plants flourish among the ancient stone
buttresses of the Pompeian Wall of the Italianate
Gardens of Hever Castle, in Kent.

greater aesthetic impact than the actual flow of water.

When designing any water feature, an important point to consider is whether you wish the container or the water to be the focal point. A great deal depends on climate. As a general rule, an ornate container in the mediaeval or renaissance style will be suitable in a hot climate, where it emphasizes the luxury of water. Indeed every single drop is precious, trapping light and magnifying it, thereby balancing, to a degree, the size of the container. In a cooler climate, where rainfall is a regular occurrence and water is not a luxury, a single drop of water will be insignificant and the container may seem irrelevant.

ISLAMIC RESTRAINT

The detail of Islamic water features seems very simple at first glance, but on close inspection shows great sophistication. The fine lines, scalloped grooves and graceful forms are designed to enhance the quality of moving water. The carved lotus flower fountain, for example, is a beautiful, but restrained design. The edging around the pool at the Court of Myrtles is another fine example of this type of restraint. It gives a unity of purpose to the overall design and brings out a quality of architectural stillness in the water, so that it harmonizes with the solid building material around it. This relationship is repeated in the negligible difference between the water level and the paving that surrounds it.

The edging also serves to exaggerate the sense of geometric perfection in the courtyard, where a horizontal plane of water complements the vertical buildings around the pool. In this way, a precise edge confirms water as part of a formal architectural ensemble. This kind of pool should always be kept brim-full, or the solid architectural effect will be marred. The space between the edging and the water level will be doubled by its own reflection, which will make the level of water in the pond look even lower than it already is.

The border of the *parterre d'eau* at Versailles, however, raises the water above ground level, holding it up to the sky to maximize its reflection, and create an uninterrupted relationship between earth and sky. It differs from the raised Islamic pools partly in that its edge is garlanded with eight statues and partly because it is not enclosed within a courtyard. The water becomes a medium to trap light. This technique is effective in climates with the low cloud ceiling typical of northern countries.

The aquaduct at the Old Mill House, in
Nottinghamshire, spans the hushed calm of the
sunlit River Poulter.

SPACE AND SERENITY

At Stourhead the containment of water looks completely natural. The slopes run down gently to the water, apparently without artificial intervention; the graceful contours of the shoreline cradle the peaceful waters of the lake. The gradient, which one always assumes continues at the same degree under water as above it, is most important because it indicates depth. Consequently a steep gradient would suggest a deep pool and a shallow gradient, a shallow pool. It is always worth observing this rule when designing a pool, especially an informal one. Remember that a gentle gradient will give a greater sense of space than a steep gradient because it will create less shadow. A minimum of shadow gives the water a greater surface to reflect light. In the English tradition, passive water emphasizes the shape and volume of water and should give an impression of space.

One of the most powerful impressions water can create is an atmosphere of calm and serenity. This does not necessarily depend on informal containment. In the Court of the Myrtles water takes up most of the available courtyard space, but the visitor nevertheless experiences a peaceful feeling. This ambience will depend on the depth of water, which if too shallow will look absurd, and if too deep, can become oppressive. This impression of space can be very welcome in a small town garden, where the limitations of a rectangular walled enclosure can be cleverly overcome by a simple water feature.

PRECISE LINES, RAISED POOLS AND BORDERS

Three different types of containment can be used to achieve this. The first possibility is the Islamic style, in which the water is edged by a precise line of paving. This will be effective if the water feature is to be stylistically linked to the house, so that the water becomes absorbed into the spirit of the architecture — as in the Court of Myrtles, where the water looks like a sheet of glass. Neither the paving nor shape need have a regular geometric pattern and a variety of different materials and shapes can be used. To reinforce a link with the house, however, it is best to find a compatible material and a shape that suits the style of the building.

The second possibility is a raised pool. This can be built either with man-made materials, such as brick, or with natural materials such as rough stone. My own feeling is that as it can never hope to integrate into natural surroundings like an informal pool, it should be treated formally with man-made materials. The raised pool is a perfect solution to a dark, enclosed garden because it will attract light. Such conditions, in which there

The circular pool at Hidcote, in Gloucestershire,
set serenely in a framework of hedges and trees.

is little natural sunlight, will not be ideal for aquatic plants, so it is best to concentrate on exploiting all the reflective possibilities of the pool. Consider water as you would a mirror glinting in a dark room: it reflects what little light creeps in through the window.

An alternative form of containment is a landscaped border. Naturally, a slope and plants will require more space and light than in the previous types, and it might therefore be less suitable for a town garden. However, even if your garden is not large, you can achieve a landscaped look: either miniaturize the scale of the pool by careful plant selection, as in the Japanese style; or keep an informal shape of pool, but dispense with the slope.

REFLECTION

Reflection is one of the great joys of passive water, as sound is of active water. Water's reflective properties can be employed to achieve a wide range of effects. The magnificence of the Taj Mahal stands in contrast to the seeming veneration of the reflections in the surrounding pools. In China, the reflection of the moon in the pond is said to be the gateway to a mermaid's palace. Similarly, great importance was attached to arched bridges — since in China the circle is a symbol of heaven — and if the water level was just right, the bridge together with its reflection would appear to form a perfect circle.

Although edging is not essential to a reflected image in water, it can enhance the effect as a frame can a picture. This technique is used in many Islamic gardens, where the interplay of object and reflection produces magical results. The effect is particularly striking when the building is colourful, with intricate textual detail, as in the gardens of Isfahan, in Iran. Here the reflective action is reciprocal — often the reflection of light on the water creates a vivid shimmering on the walls of the building.

When water is placed in close proximity to a building, light will play an important part in the relationship between the two. Depending on its position, the building and the water can be lit separately by the sun. The intriguing contrast of dark water and light building, or vice versa, is often exploited by landscape designers and architects.

Consider, for example, the aesthetic impact of a dark, looming castle surrounded by the opaque rill of its moat or, in contrast, a high-tech, glinting glass building and the water in front of it like a slab of black, polished marble. This *chiaroscuro* effect will depend more on the positioning of the building than on its texture.

Pink, purple and red primulas add a rich beauty to
the waterside at Longstock on a dewy morning.

REFLECTIONS ON YOUR POOL

Reflection is such an important aspect of still water that it is a great pity not to make the most of it. To do this you will have to consider both the positioning and size of the pool. Reflections will be most varied if the pool is sited near the house. Clouds, vegetation or a sculpture will be reflected when looking from inside the house; and when looking at the pool from the garden, the image of the house itself will be seen.

Bear in mind that height will also make a big difference. The Islamic pools were placed low because they were often viewed from a seated position. An important point to remember is that the reflection will only be effective if the base of the pool is black. A white base has quite different properties, causing the water to sparkle more, but making reflections look faded and muted.

A light-coloured finish — normally white or sky blue — is often used in municipal fountains and swimming pools, and this colouring has great artistic possibilities. David Hockney, for example, has painted wonderfully effective ripple-patterns at the bottom of a swimming pool. With the right paint and a little initiative you can make a pattern at the bottom of your water feature. As an alternative, try making a mosaic pattern with treated bricks or stones. However, light-coloured finishes have their disadvantages; nothing is more displeasing than the sight of rotting leaves and debris accumulating at the bottom of a swimming pool in autumn and winter.

Finally, remember that reflection works better if the surface of the water is free from plants. If you wish to have aquatics, they should be planted sparingly. Alternatively, opt for reeds along the border: these will stand upright, and make a pleasant contrast with the glassy reflections in a still pool.

The design of any passive water feature will depend to a large extent on climate and geography. Nevertheless, personal taste as to the form a passive water feature should take, also plays an important part in the initial design concept. By observing some of the above principles, the water garden designer will reach a greater understanding of this very versatile medium.

This modern treatment of the traditional *tsukubai*
is relieved by the delicacy of the bamboo pipe
that feeds it, and the careful arrangement of the
plants.

MOVING WATER

CASCADES AND WATERFALLS

While still water evokes a sense of serenity and space, moving water possesses altogether different qualities: vitality and life. And in the same way that reflection is a property of still water, sound is a property of moving water. Water creates a variety of sounds: the resonance of a single drop; the comforting murmur of a stream; or the splash of falling water. There is music for every mood.

The Moghuls were the pioneers of the formal use of large quantities of moving water, building wide cascades in their gardens in Kashmir. Through skilful design, the raw material was transformed into effervescent white sheets and fine mists of spray, from which all the colours of the rainbow unfolded. Designers have made great use of the refractive and reflective properties of the surface of water, changing light in the same way as a prism. When illuminated by direct sunlight, the effervescence of a foaming white cascade can produce a superb effect. The *chadar* cascade in Kashmir is an example of this art at the peak of its perfection; there is a magical fusion of water, energy, air, sound and light.

The *chadar* is a veil of water laid on marble carved into a thousand scalloped shells or prisms. The water courses down the marble slope, churned up and aerated by tiny air pockets until it looks like a white crystalline sheet. The Sicilian poet Ibn Hamdis described it in rapturous terms in 1132: "Waters are like ingots of silver which meet on the steps of the *Shadirwan*".

When building a waterfall, a variety of techniques can be utilized to create unusual effects. Velocity is important, as is the edge over which the water falls. Curling edges, for example, will create a curtain-like cascade. If the edge is crenellated, the water will be divided into separate jets. At Chatsworth, in Derbyshire, at least five different kinds of lip create different falls of water. In Kashmir, the Moghuls again demonstrated their aesthetic skills in their treatment of transparent sheets of water; they carved niches, called *chinikinas*, into the wall behind a curtain of water. At night candles

The arc of this pool's edge, surrounded by paving,
gives the garden, the work of Japanese gardener
Inoue, an almost sculptural quality.

flickered in the niches and during the day the candles were replaced by golden vases planted with silver flowers. This idea should be easily within the grasp of the amateur designer and with careful planning, should make an original and successful water feature.

In Italy, moving water was seen as a joyful expression of vitality and life. The Italians' sense of freedom and fun was borne out by countless tricks and gimmicks involving water. One amusing and eye-catching water feature is the *ovato* at the Villa d'Este, designed by Ligoria. Drawing on the idea of the water curtain in the Moghul garden, the *ovato* is essentially a semi-circular waterfall behind which people can walk and experience the wonderful sensation of looking at the world through glistening sheets of water. The scale of this trick makes it difficult for the amateur to achieve the effect, but it is not impossible.

THE NATURAL WATERFALL

It was the power of the natural waterfall that inspired the American architect Frank Lloyd Wright. His masterly, *Falling Water* is a house designed to project over a natural waterfall. The unceasing flow of water unifies the house with its natural environment, so that it becomes a harmonious part of the surrounding rock strata and foliage. Dappled by the play of light, *Falling Water* is a prime example of how water can be used to bridge the gap between architectural design and natural form.

Waterfalls similarly inspired American designer Lawrence Halprin, whose major works include the Auditorium Forecourt Fountain and the Lovejoy Plaza in Portland, Oregon. Both are immense theatres of water, expressing the essential ruggedness and brutality of water in a thoroughly modernistic way: water gushes and streams in cascades and waterfalls from the top terraces to a pool.

In Japan, however, moving water is treated in a more reserved fashion. The main aim behind a Japanese waterfall is that it should imitate and idealize nature and not appear artificial. In the Japanese vocabulary a number of metaphorical terms describe the different characteristics of waterfalls: *nuno-ochi* is a white cloth hanging down; *ito-ochi* is a screen of thread; a *sayu-ochi* means falling from right to left; and a *kasane-ochi*, falling in two or three stages.

Although the desired effect was one of informality, Japanese garden designers were always aware of a number of constraints. Like all features in the Japanese garden, the design of a waterfall conformed to a set of rules. Sometimes, as in the Sanzon Ishigumi, the waterfall symbolized the unity of

Maples and evergreens form a delightful setting
for the zig-zag bridge and stone lanterns of this
Japanese-style garden at Tatton Park, in Cheshire.

three figures in Buddhist belief. Alternatively, the reference was to a natural phenomenon: the pointed rock at the foot of a waterfall, for example, which hints at the vibrant form of a leaping carp.

FOUNTAINS

The fountain adds another dimension to moving water. Unlike the waterfall, the fountain is rarely a natural phenomenon, but the fact that it is man-made means that more often than not it becomes the focal point of the composition. Buildings, open spaces and garden foliage are put in perspective by a fountain, so that however many disparate elements are featured in a landscape design, the overall effect will be one of visual unity.

Until the 20th century, the fountain played an important role in society. It marked the centrepoint in towns and villages, where people could gather to exchange local gossip and collect water; but the siege of our squares by hectic traffic and the installation of municipal water supplies have both contributed to its demise. As a result, the aesthetic principles behind fountain design no longer have to be tempered by practical concerns.

But, ironically, it has recently been discovered that the fountain is beneficial to the physiological and psychological health of city dwellers. Water falling in the form of rain, waterfalls and fountains generates a negative static charge — or ionization — that attracts positively charged particles such as carbon dioxide. These particles, which are thought to have a depressant effect, are concentrated in urban areas. The running water of a fountain catches the particles in the water and deposits them in a filter system. So perhaps the civic fountain will take on a new lease of life.

FOUNTAINS AS SYMBOLS AND IN RELIGION

There are many different types of fountain, but one particularly interesting example is the Japanese *tsukubai*. This usually takes the form of a round stone basin of clear water. The basin is constantly replenished by water, which drips slowly but regularly from a length of bamboo pipe. The *tsukubai* has both a symbolic and a functional place in the Japanese garden; on the one hand it represents purity and simplicity; on the other, the water is scooped up with a bamboo ladle to cleanse the hands before the tea ceremony.

Islamic fountain design is similarly restrained, as the fountain serves a religious purpose and is mainly used for ritual ablutions before prayer. Unlike the *tsukubai*, however, which blends harmoniously into the garden composition, the Islamic fountain is designed to stand out against its

The sense of formal containment given by the
paved border of this pool at Faringdon House is
set off by the delightfully informal – almost
surrealist-effect of the statue.

surroundings, a refreshing contrast to the heat and dust of a hot climate. The water is often forced upwards through a central spout: this is different again from Oriental custom, in which water normally flows downwards.

THE FOUNTAIN AS ART

The European fountains of the Renaissance were pieces of sculpture in their own right. Some of the best examples can be found at the Villa d'Este, in Italy, where, among many choreographic uses of water and many fountains sculpted in human form, there stands a remarkable sculpture of Diane of the Ephesians offering a bountiful supply of water through her multiple breasts. The Trevi fountain in Rome, built in 1762 by Salvi, is a fine example of Baroque sculpture. Its fluid lines give the illusion of movement and the statues are animated by the luminosity, vitality and sound of water.

The idea of using water to express light, movement and sound in sculpture was interpreted in a very different way in the Constructivist movement at the beginning of the century. In it, moving water represented space. The pioneer of Constructivist art, Naum Gabo, believed that the emphasis in art should be on space rather than mass. In his revolving sculpture at St. Thomas's Hospital, in London, Gabo represents the space occupied by a three-dimensional circle through the interplay of light and water. By changing its spatial relationship to its surroundings, it becomes dissociated from volume and mass.

But perhaps the most compelling characteristic of a fountain is its fascinating cyclical transformation. The water is expelled under great pressure upwards into the air before spraying outwards and falling in showers. As it falls, a powdery spray of tiny drops is framed for a second, before shattering the water surface. This process continuously repeats itself: the crystalline column; the dancing plume; the feathery mist — all change the character of the water surface from a flat, passive mirror to a vibrant, active plane.

Today, modern technology has added a new dimension to what was already a multi-dimensional form. Different nozzles can be used to create a myriad of complex spray patterns, and time clocks and electronic controls can be used to change sets of nozzles and choreograph a kaleidoscopic splendour of effects. But it is important that one is not too distracted by these tricks: water design in the past has been successful mainly because it has had a spiritual and contemplative purpose underlying a visual attraction.

The skilful placing and vital shapes of the rocks
add spirit and animation to this carefully contrived
stream setting, designed by Ken Nakajima.

WATER GARDEN TECHNIQUES

Formal or informal; Planting and Protection;
What kind of pool?; Shape; Depth; Pool Liners and
Pre-formed Pools; Installation; Edging and Paving;
Building a Bog Garden; Fountains; Waterfalls;
Tsukubai; What Type of Water Feature?; Lighting;
Fish; Planting and Maintenance; Plant Listings.

INDEX and ACKNOWLEDGEMENTS

Stourhead, in Avon, laid out by the Hoare family in
the mid-18th century, spearheaded the
development of the English landscape tradition.

FORMAL OR INFORMAL

Introducing a water feature into a garden will breathe new life into it, giving its components, its trees and open spaces, or in a smaller garden, its boundaries and borders, a new visual appeal. In a sense, it dramatizes physical relationships. For this reason it should be handled with confidence and purpose.

The design of a pool is the first and most important step in its creation. Like all design, this includes style; function and desired effect. There are, of course many different styles of pool, but, basically they fall into two broad categories. These are the formal and the informal. Although it is possible to combine the two styles, an informal pool within a formal context or a formal pool within an informal context — this runs the risk of creating a basic

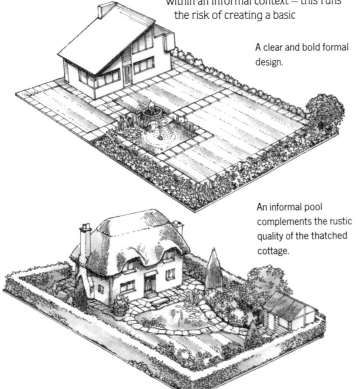

A clear and bold formal design.

An informal pool complements the rustic quality of the thatched cottage.

incompatibility. Therefore when making choices about design, bear in mind the type of home you live in, whether it is a thatched cottage in the country or a modern town house. This consideration will also affect the decision you will have to make as to where you site the pool.

If the pool is to be located near the house, it ought to enhance and dramatize its architectural style. It is possible to juxtapose the energy and severe lines of much modern architecture with the smooth contours of an informal pool. But this would be difficult to achieve with a small pool in a small garden, where it might look diminutive and out of place. It is quite simply a question of scale. In most cases, where the size of the house is relatively much larger than the area taken up by the pool, a geometric house with sharp, crisp lines should be complemented by a formal pool.

If on the other hand you wish to site the pool at some distance from the house, an informal pool might be more suitable. A pool placed at the end of the garden, not visible from the house, will be an interesting discovery on a walk through the garden. Generally, though, the aesthetic and horticultural potential of a garden can be best exploited if the pool is a focal point in the garden.

Unlike the formal pool, the informal pool should not echo modern architectural style. Instead it should suggest a feeling of permanence, of having been formed before the house was built, and in this way it signifies a satisfying link with nature.

PLANTING AND PROTECTION

Having decided on the shape, size and site of the pool, the next question to consider is that of planting. Firstly, should the pool contain planting or not? Beautiful pools exist both with and without plants. There are a few fundamental points to bear in mind. Most aquatic plants will not thrive in the vicinity of fountains or waterfalls, as they dislike turbulence. So if the pond is small, it might not be wise to incorporate a waterfall, or fountain, as well as plants.

Ideally, in order to cultivate healthy aquatics, your pool should fulfill two conditions. It must receive the maximum amount of sun, so ensuring robust growth of plants and optimum flowering and secondly, it should be protected from the wind, which otherwise will snap the tall stems of marginal plants. Preferably the location should be south-facing, with protection from the northerly wind. This protection can be provided by the house or trees. It is important, however, not to site the pool too close to deciduous trees, unless the leaves can be raked out or prevented from falling into the water. Debris from fallen leaves, seeds and twigs will decay and cause pollution. Leaves from holly, laurel and horse chestnut are poisonous and the laburnum highly so. You should also be wary of poplars and willows, however attractive they may appear, as they contain aspirin.

Although the garden designer often hesitates at first about siting a pool in the proximty of the house, this is often the best position. Not only will the house protect the pool from the wind, but you will be able to enjoy the special beauties of the pool from inside your home: the view of slowly unfolding leaves and buds, the shooting flames of fish and dragonflies and the reflections of the changing skies are an unending source of delight.

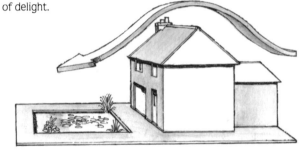

In the winter, the surface is transformed by the low winter light and sometimes it will freeze over. These variations in the appearance of the water are infinitely compelling. Remember also that in the summer or winter, the steely glint and glass-like texture of the water will emphasize textures and colours in the garden proper. For this reason alone, it is a good idea to place the pool in the line of view from a window.

The ideal site for a pool is a sunny location, sheltered either by the house or by strategically-placed planting. Aquatic plants will achieve optimum performance if the pool is located in a sunny spot with protection from the wind.

WHAT KIND OF POOL?

Raised pools have certain advantages over sunken ones. Although the former can never look totally natural, they can add a distinct touch of style to your garden. In a wet climate, the continual replenishment of a raised pool by rainfall creates an irregular silver patina of raindrops on the water surface, while clouds cause ever-changing reflections. These transformations give the raised pool enormous aesthetic potential. Also, by its very nature, the raised pool gives a greater impression of the physical mass and quantity of water; its containment becomes more significant.

The disadvantage of raised pools is their susceptibility to temperature changes. Artificial insulation certainly helps, but it never matches the stability of earth temperature. The raised pool is perhaps more difficult and expensive to construct, requiring some knowledge of both concrete- and brick-laying, but nothing that could not be mastered by the enthusiastic amateur.

The sunken pool provides ideal conditions for all kinds of vegetation, including a bog garden. The earth that has been dug up can be used to create a mound on which you can build a waterfall and introduce further planting.

The art of creating sunken pools was perfected by the Japanese, who included bridges and islands to reproduce an exquisite miniature of the natural landscape. Glimmering lanterns in these quiet gardens give anyone who enters them a feeling that he or she is entering a fantasy world.

The emphasis in the English water garden is different. Its beauty lies in the luxuriant and colourful growth of a rich variety of aquatic plants. To create this sort of garden you will need to acquire a knowledge of different types of plants and their individual needs.

A more formal water garden can offer a surprising range of possible designs. The severity of geometrical lines might appear stark and unnatural to some, but this can be offset by intelligent planting. The handsome leaves of some aquatic plants make an inviting contrast to the precise lines of the pool.

A raised pool can provide a pleasant seating area in the garden.
One advantage of a sunken pool is that it is less susceptible to fluctuations in temperature and guarantees better plant-performance.

SHAPE

A common mistake when designing a pool is to make the shape too complicated. The most obvious disadvantage is that it is harder to build a pool with a complicated shape than it is to build one with a simple shape. There are, however, other problems. Remember, you will never appreciate the view of the garden from an aerial perspective. Therefore the elaborate design on paper will be distorted when looked at straight on. A convoluted design will make the garden appear cluttered. As the plants mature, a "tight" construction may be choked up, losing the comforting glint of water and the shape of the contours. The best policy is to stick to a simple shape.

One of the most efficient ways of deciding on a particular shape is to use a length of rope or hosepipe as an outline for the pool. Take into account the areas which will be in the shade and those in sunlight. Bear in mind that hardy water-lilies will require at least four hours of direct sunlight a day and tropical water-lilies at least five or six. The size should be proportional to the size of the house, garden and other garden features. Even at this early stage, it is important to consider which properties of water you wish to exploit. Every garden has some inherent potential, which a water feature can highlight. A sensitivity to natural form and the different aspects of the garden go a long way towards creating a successful water feature.

By experimenting with the rope or hosepipe, you can get a fair idea of the size of the pool. It is best to make this as large as possible, given the amount of space available overall. The bigger the pool, the more chance it has of achieving a self-sustained ecological balance. This requires a certain stability in temperature, which will be forfeited if the pool is small.

When planning a pool, bear in mind that it will look different when looked at straight on than when seen from above.

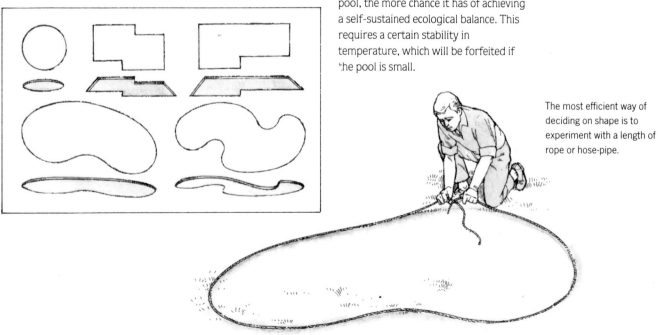

The most efficient way of deciding on shape is to experiment with a length of rope or hose-pipe.

DEPTH

Having decided on the location and general shape of the pool, construction can begin. Here, it is important to understand how depth can affect the health of aquatic plants and fish. Although the pool should be as large as possible – within the limits of your

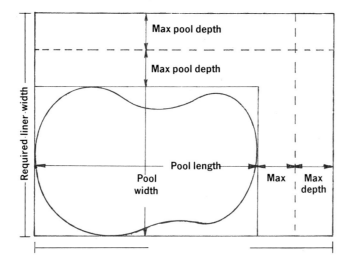

Use this plan to calculate the amount of lining material you will need.

garden – it will rarely be necessary to dig deeper than two feet (60 centimetres).

Depth can be calculated according to the volume of water. If the surface area of the pond is not counterbalanced by adequate depth the pond will overheat. Consequently the water will quickly become a breeding ground for algae, that chokes plants and discolours the water. These problems can be avoided provided the volume of water is adequate. You should aim for at least ten gallons per square foot (490 litres per square metre) – seven (318 litres) at the minimum. A pool with a surface area

of 40 foot square should never be less than 15 inches deep. (A pool with a surface area of 4 metres square should never be less than 38 centimetres deep). This means that one square foot will have eight gallons of water beneath it (one square metre should have 380 litres). Anything less than eight gallons per square foot (or 380 litres per square metre) will jeopardise the ecological stability of the pool and discolour the water. If the depth is 24 inches (60 centimetres), every square foot (square metre) of water will constitute 12.5 gallons (600 litres). This would be an excellent depth.

A pool larger than 40 foot square (or four metres square) should be at least 18 inches (45 centimetres) deep and, if over 100 foot square (or 10 metres square), it should be at least 24 inches (60 centimetres) deep. This constitutes 12.5 gallons (600 litres) per square foot which is an ideal volume/surface ratio.

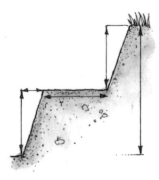

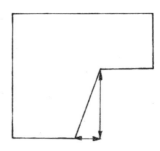

When you have decided the depth of your pool and worked out the angle of slope (*top*), make a template of hardboard or wood to those dimensions (*middle*). Then use this to ensure precise measurments when digging (*bottom*).

POOL LINERS AND PRE-FORMED POOLS

There are a number of different ways of building a pool. Before the advent of concrete and liners, pools were waterproofed with puddled clay, mixed with straw and "puddled" until they became impermeable. With the introduction of concrete, pre-formed pools and liners, waterproofing techniques have become much simpler.

Although it is tempting to have more faith in the strength and durability of concrete than in pre-formed pools and liners, it is possible that stress — the expansion and contraction caused by freezing for example, or by the growth of tree roots — will crack the concrete. The advantages of concrete tend to diminish when compared with a butyl or laminated PVC pool liner, which can be moulded into any shape, is unaffected by temperature fluctuation, ultra-violet rays, oxidising agents and, in the case of butyl, has a life expectancy of up to 100 years. Even if it is punctured it can be repaired.

The best butyl lining is 0.030 inches (0.8 millimetres) thick and comes in black. If the edges are well-made and the lining is not visible, black will bring out the clear reflective properties of a deep pool. If, however, you prefer a shallow effect, butyl is not suitable, so you might consider instead a laminated PVC, which comes in blue.

It is important to know the depth of the pool when calculating the size of the lining. If a pool is 10ft x 10ft x 2ft (3.05m x 3.05m x 0.60m) deep, the lining should measure 14ft x 14ft (4.27m x 4.27m). This is worked out by a simple calculation. Add twice the pond depth, in this case, 2ft x 2ft (0.60m x 0.60m) to both length and width, which makes 14ft (4.27m). If the area is 6ft x 8ft (1.83m x 2.44m) and 18in (46cm) deep, the liner will measure 9ft (2.74m), that is, (6ft + 18in + 18in) (1.83m + 46cm + 46cm) x 11ft (3.35m), that is, (8ft + 18in + 18in) (2.44m + 46cm + 46cm).

The alternative to lining is the pre-formed pool, made from either resin-bonded glass fibre or the less expensive semi-rigid plastic. If the shape, size and depth fit your design requirements, this can be the most convenient way to create a pool. It is a common mistake, however, to choose one for convenience but overlook its limitations.

When visiting a garden centre, it is difficult to envisage exactly how a pre-formed pool will look once it is installed in your garden. Often it will seem bigger seen above ground, than it will when sunk in the pool-site and disguised with plants. Another disadvantage is that you cannot create your own design, and it may be difficult to find one that fits well into the style and shape of your garden.

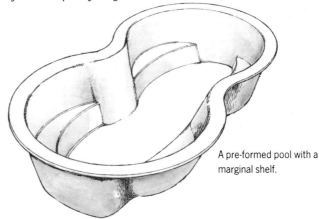

A pre-formed pool with a marginal shelf.

INSTALLATION

Whether you opt for a lining or a pre-formed pool, in both cases you should start the procedure of installing the pool with a template made from wood. This is used to check the level of the marginal shelf and the angle of the pool sides.

The pool sides should not be vertical, since, if they are, they may collapse. The optimum angle is 20 degrees to the vertical or one inch in three. If the soil crumbles easily or if it is sandy, this angle should be increased. The marginal shelf should be about ten inches (25cm) wide and nine inches (23cm) below the edge.

Before you start to dig, it is a good idea to hammer in some pegs to ensure that the sides of the pool will be level. Hammer the pegs down to the level you want the pool sides to be. Using a spirit level and a length of straight wood, make sure all the pegs are exactly the same level. This will prevent one side of the pool from being higher than the other.

Once the desired depth has been reached, any sharp objects on the pool floor should be removed as they might pierce the lining. To safeguard further against this, it is best to put down a ½ inch (12.7mm) layer of sand on the pool floor. The sloping sides can be cushioned with newspaper or roofing felt.

Next the liner can be placed over the hole. Make sure there is an even overlap on all sides, which you then weigh down all around with stones. A constant tension on the liner as it is being filled with water will ensure a minimum of

Use a length of straight wood, a spirit level and wooden pegs to ensure the pool is level.

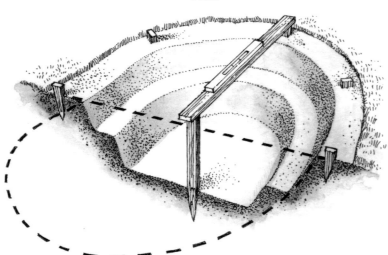

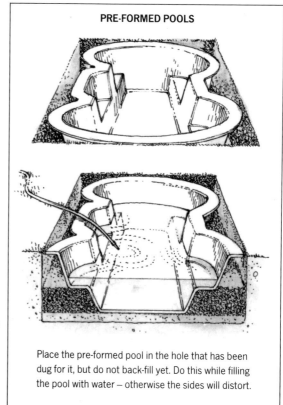

PRE-FORMED POOLS

Place the pre-formed pool in the hole that has been dug for it, but do not back-fill yet. Do this while filling the pool with water — otherwise the sides will distort.

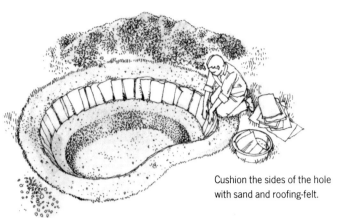

Cushion the sides of the hole with sand and roofing-felt.

creases. At any rate the creases will not be discernible when the plants have matured.

When installing a pre-formed pool, it is important to fill the gap surrounding it with earth, at the same time as you fill the pool with water. Any other method will result in distortion of the pool shape. Choose fine earth rather than coarse, and make sure that it is well pushed in to ensure support for the pool on all sides.

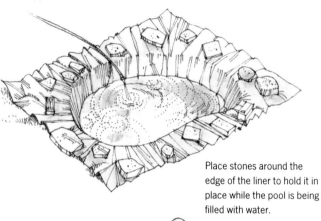

Place stones around the edge of the liner to hold it in place while the pool is being filled with water.

If the pool is raised, the retaining wall must also be lined with butyl.

It looks more attractive if the butyl is run between the two rows of bricks in the wall, but this may make the structure less stable.

A marginal shelf combined with a raised water level gives the pool another dimension.

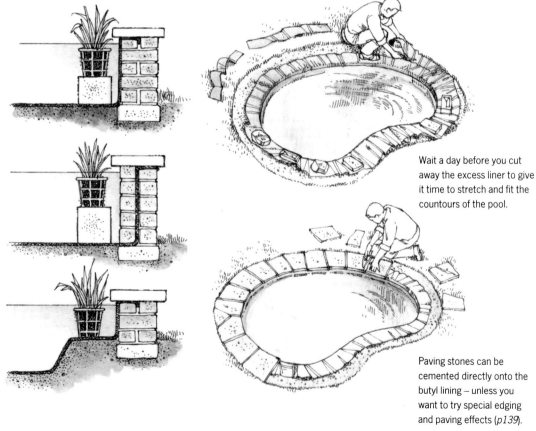

Wait a day before you cut away the excess liner to give it time to stretch and fit the countours of the pool.

Paving stones can be cemented directly onto the butyl lining – unless you want to try special edging and paving effects (*p139*).

EDGING AND PAVING

A cement foundation for the paving stone increases stability and may be essential in sandy soil. Dig a trench before digging the pool, then: **1** Fix wooden shuttering at a 20 angle. **2** Pour in the cement evenly, making sure it fills all the corners. **3** When the cement is dry, remove shuttering and dig out the pool. **4** When laying the liner, remember to leave a surplus of around 7 inches (18cm).

Building the edging is a very important stage in the construction of the pool as you will have to be aware of both its functional and aesthetic roles. Not only does the edging serve to hide the pool-lining, it also enhances the design. A very simple pool can be made to look something quite special. Edging can also be extended to form an adjacent terrace or, in the case of an informal garden, it can be made to look like a natural slope.

Once the pool is full, the surplus liner should be removed, but remember to leave about 7 inches (18cm) around all the sides. You must be certain that the weight of the water takes up all the

liner, so wait a day or two before cutting it. Once cut, the paving stones can be cemented directly on to the lining. To ensure the paving stones are quite stable, it is best to use large ones, at least 20 inches square (131 centimetres square). Do not forget that you will need a 3-inch (7.6cm) overlap to hide the lining and protect it from the sun. (The overlap also helps to give the pool a look of depth and mystery). The paving should be cemented using a three-part sand to one-part cement mortar. If you want the water to come right up to the paving stones you would do well to mix in an impermeabilising

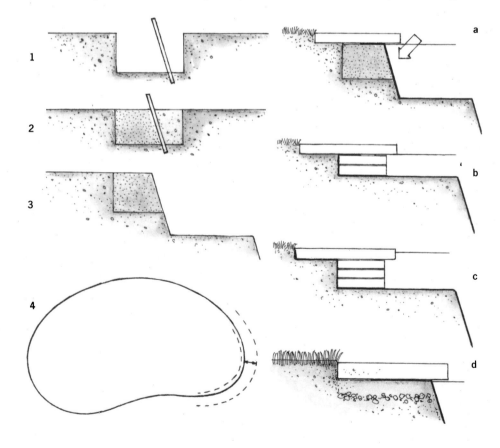

a Position the paving stone so that it just overhangs the water, and protect the cement with the liner.
b For extra protection, wrap the butyl liner round the foundation; if the water level is to be above the foundation, **c**, wrap the underside of the paving stone in liner, too, but if you decide to do this, remember to leave more excess liner before cutting it.
d Planting will help to camouflage the liner when it reaches behind the paving stone.

agent, otherwise the water will leak through the cement. A basic rule to follow is that any cement that will come into contact with water should be treated with either a rubberized paint, or a special chemical, such as *Silglaze*.

If you do not wish to have edging around the pool, you may prefer to build a gentle slope instead. Remember that the angle of the slope will reflect the depth of the pool. A shallow slope suggests a shallow pool and a deeper slope suggests a deeper one. To achieve a perfect balance in which the pool blends in harmoniously with its surroundings you will have to take time to experiment. Remember that planting will make a difference and this should be taken into account when deciding on the angle of the slope.

Interesting paving stones can turn a simple pool into something quite special, as well as hiding ugly linings. Included below are: a variety of brick-patterns, crazy paving, cobble stones and circular slabs nestling in plants.

BUILDING A
BOG GARDEN

A bog garden is an ideal way of creating a pleasant transition between water and land. As well as providing an interesting visual link in your garden design, it will also give your garden greater horticultural variety. This includes a profusion of weeds. Bog garden plants differ from aquatic plants because their roots need air, so it is one of the great advantages of lining that it makes this possible.

Bog gardens are suitable for both formal and informal pools. A formal pool can be complemented by building a dividing wall at each end creating two narrow beds. A bog garden for an informal pool should bring out the inherent contours, but this might be difficult after the pool has been made. A bog garden can be built inside or outside the main pool, simultaneously or after its construction, though this has its disadvantages with an informal pool, as stated above. If it is created at the same time, it is a question of sculpting a dividing mound which should then be covered by liner and topped with stone.

If the bog garden is created after the construction of the main pool, a retaining wall must be built, using bricks and mortar, which allows water to permeate through. Since this wall will not have deep, strong foundations, it should have a broad base to prevent it

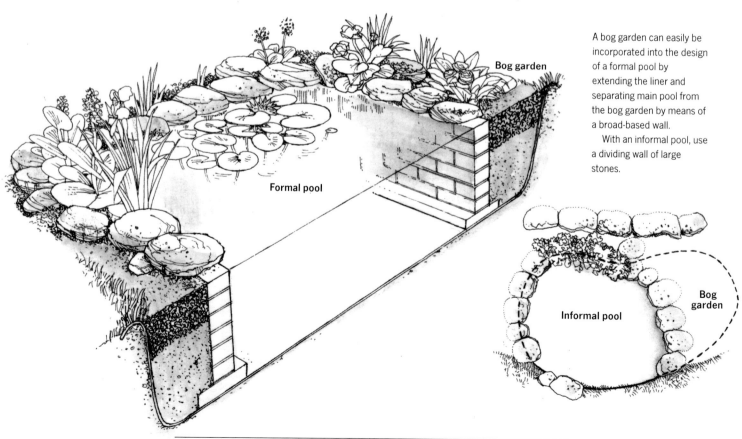

A bog garden can easily be incorporated into the design of a formal pool by extending the liner and separating main pool from the bog garden by means of a broad-based wall.

With an informal pool, use a dividing wall of large stones.

Bog garden

Formal pool

Informal pool

Bog garden

evaporation that occurs through the bog garden. This means the water level of the main pool will be lowered, so the water will have to be continually replenished. In general, therefore, it is not advisable to build a bog garden in a shallow pool.

A possibly more effective bog garden can be created by digging a completely separate hole, about 18 inches (44cm) deep, next to the main pool. This should be lined with a polythene liner, perforated to prevent saturation and water stagnation, which will sour the earth. Lay 6 inches (15cm) of gravel around a hosepipe perforated with holes 24 inches (60cm) apart. Make sure that the holes are not too big and are regularly sized, as otherwise irrigation will be uneven. The pipe should be sealed at one end with the other end exposed. During summer months it is simple business connecting the hose pipe to a tap and irrigating the bog garden.

A bog garden should have 12 inches (30cm) of soil. If it is to be within the main pool, a bank will have to be built to allow aeration of the roots. The soil mixture should consist of one half loam, or seasoned compost mould, a quarter coarse-grained sand – from two to five millimetres in size to allow permeation – and the rest should be well-rotted cow manure and peat.

Perforate the hose pipe supplying the bog garden with regularly spaced holes, to ensure an even supply of water throughout the area.

collapsing. The wall should be built on a pool liner, which should be protected, using roofing felt or liner. Take care to treat the mortar with *Silglaze* before filling the pool with water as otherwise pollution may result. The bog garden within the main pool is an often criticised technique, because the water of the main pool frequently becomes muddied. Building the wall too high in order to prevent this, is not a solution however, as there will not be enough water to saturate the garden. Another disadvantage is the considerable

FOUNTAINS

Since the earliest gardens, man has sought ways of creating waterfalls and fountains to celebrate the many properties of water. Nowadays, with the help of modern technology, the delight and charm of these special water features are available to everyone with a garden.

In some cases, however, the pool might not be suitable for either waterfall or fountain. Remember that aquatic plants, for example, dislike water currents, and should not be in the proximity of moving water. So, unless the pool is large enough to accommodate both water feature and aquatics, or a separate rim can be installed, a choice has to be made.

You should also consider how the water feature will fit in with the rest of your garden design. The fountain, for example, is an artificial device with a symmetrical spray and it is not always possible to adapt it to informal surroundings. Scale is also an important aspect. A small fountain might be

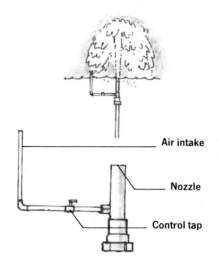

Air intake

Nozzle

Control tap

An aerated jet creates a low mound of foaming water.

This mushroom jet has a plunger that can be adjusted to vary the height and width of the cascade.

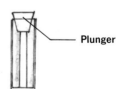

Plunger

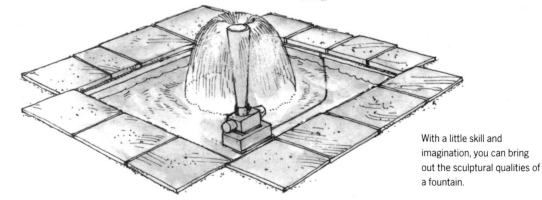

With a little skill and imagination, you can bring out the sculptural qualities of a fountain.

depressing in a wet climate, but in a hot climate, the spray is easily evaporated and this causes wastage.

An interesting aspect of the fountain is that it brings out an architectural quality in water. For this reason it often combines well with a hard material like stone.

Modern technology has revolutionized the fountain. Different nozzles can be fitted, that produce a variety of spray patterns. You can buy tinted lenses, which rotate at different speeds, creating kaleidescopic patterns of colour in the water. This technique is particularly effective at night.

Though very spectacular, this kind of fountain will not always fit into the surroundings. It should always be borne in mind that the spirit of water lies in its natural beauty. While special effects, if employed with care and thought, can enhance this beauty, it would be a pity to decorate a water feature like a Christmas tree.

One of the most important practical concerns is the positioning of the fountain. Unless you are careful, wind will blow the spray beyond the perimeter of the pool and create a dangerous, slippery surface on paving, as well as depleting the volume of water in the pool. In order to avoid this, you should ensure that the diameter of the pool is at least twice the height of the jet, and at least four times in windy areas. In the latter case, a straight, columnar jet is never achievable and it would be better to opt for a different form of fountain altogether.

Maintaining a fountain with a small orifice — of the sort that creates a columnar jet — is not always simple, as the smaller the orifice, the more susceptible it is to clogging up. A fountain with a larger aperture produces a lower spray, which falls over a larger area, and is unlikely to become blocked.

Two interesting and unusual designs from Germany show the range of possibilities when building a fountain. One blends traditional and modern (*above*), with water spouting from a pipe into a crude stone basin; the other (*left*) uses high-tech stainless steel discs to obtain its effect.

WATERFALLS

In terms of construction, a waterfall can be divided into a series of descending basins. By planning in this way, each stage of the cascade will provide an individual focus for the eye, while there are other advantages as well. The basins will force the water to pause before each fall, so that the flow leaves the spill edge with constant velocity.

The spill edge is also important visually, as it will shape the form of the falling water. If a jagged surface is used, for example, the sheet will be broken and fragmented. If the surface is fluted, the falling water will be divided into a striated pattern of light and dark.

It is important that the water breaks cleanly with the surface, especially when small quantities of water and slow velocity are involved. Otherwise it will dribble unsatisfactorily and never form a steady sheet. There are two ways of avoiding this. Either the lip can be made of a strip of perspex or metal, which juts out slightly beyond the spill edge, or, the underside of the waterfall can be notched to force a break with the surface tension.

By creating an overhang for each waterfall, you can also amplify the sound of the falling water. The steps of the waterfall should be between 6 and 12in (15 + 30cm) high. If they are any lower neither the sound, nor the vertical movement of the water can be fully appreciated. Experiment with the velocity of the water and plant a rock at the foot of the fall onto which the water can splash. The result will be a pleasant musical sound to back up the waterfall's visual impact and in Japan, indeed, waterfalls are sometimes "tuned" by specialists.

Remember that the higher the source of the waterfall, the stronger the pump required to raise the water. Before deciding on its height it is worth visiting a

The spill edge shapes the flow of water.
A flat edge works better if it has a notch in its under-surface, causing the water to fall freely.
A curling edge creates a sheet flow.

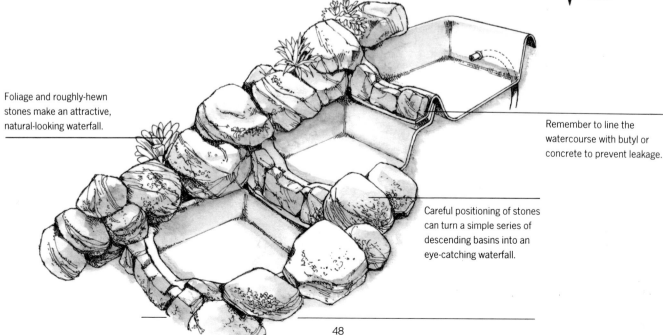

Foliage and roughly-hewn stones make an attractive, natural-looking waterfall.

Remember to line the watercourse with butyl or concrete to prevent leakage.

Careful positioning of stones can turn a simple series of descending basins into an eye-catching waterfall.

pump specialist. The waterfall course should be lined with butyl or concrete, and great care should be taken that it is impermeable. If the liner allows any leakage, the water in the pool that is being recycled will gradually be depleted.

To guarantee efficient waterproofing, it is best to build a reinforced concrete foundation several inches thick, which runs from the source to the pool. Rocks and stones can be added onto this base. As an alternative, butyl can be used, and the stones can be cemented directly onto it. It is also possible to buy moulded glass fibre waterfalls at a water garden centre.

As with a fountain, it is easy to misjudge the correct scale of a waterfall in relation to the garden. To create a sensation of visual depth, place small or angular stones in the background. Like this you can achieve the effect of a fast-flowing mountain stream. Stones in the foreground should be larger and more rounded. You can heighten the visual appeal of a waterfall by conjuring up different moods at different stages.

To create the least possible disturbance to plants the total volume of water per hour should equal the volume of water in the pond. Although twice the volume is acceptable, this will affect the health of the plants. Be careful that the amount of water corresponds to the size of the waterfall. A thin trickle threading its way between large rocks will not be very impressive.

Bearing in mind that the pump will probably not be working all the time, the waterfall should look attractive even when not operative. Perhaps the best way to do this is to create lips for each basin, so ensuring that water remains in them. Liberal sprinklings of gravel will give a textural contrast to the waterfall, even when it is not working. A covering of gravel will also protect the lining from the sun and prolong its life.

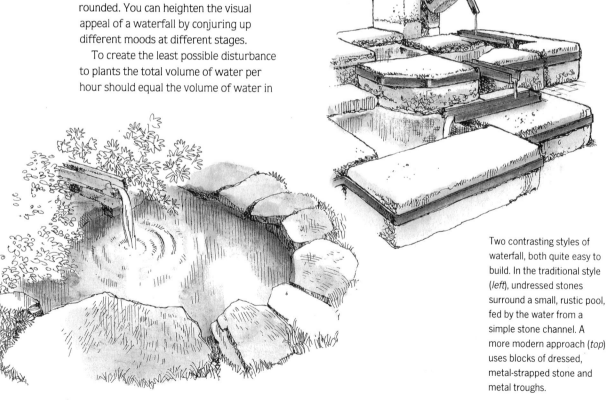

Two contrasting styles of waterfall, both quite easy to build. In the traditional style (*left*), undressed stones surround a small, rustic pool, fed by the water from a simple stone channel. A more modern approach (*top*) uses blocks of dressed, metal-strapped stone and metal troughs.

TSUKUBAI

A *tsukubai* plays an important part in the Japanese tea-ceremony, but can make an attractive feature in any garden. It can be made from a pillar, a millstone or a hollowed-out rock.

The Japanese *tsukubai* is essentially a stone basin, filled with water and placed beside the path leading to the tea-ceremony house. Washing one's hands in an act of self-purification is one of the integral stages of the ceremony. The idea is similar to the use of holy water in Christian churches.

Nowadays, the tea-ceremony is an exercise in spiritual-training, the purpose of which is to give the participant a heightened perception of beauty. This is achieved through a long and delicate ritual, which is structured around the drinking of a special kind of tea.

Any vessel can be used for the *tsukubai*, though to remain true to the spirit of the ceremony, it should evoke a certain aura of dignity and solemnity. In Japan, such

vessels include foundation- pillars and millstones or hollowed-out rocks. The vessel should be at least 6 inches deep and the water should always be clean.

To appreciate the tea-ceremony fully, it should be approached with an attitude of humility. For this reason, the *tsukubai* is placed low on the ground so that, regardless of social standing, all participants have to stoop down to cleanse themselves. Crouching down on the first stone, which is placed before the vessel, the acolyte reaches out for the bamboo ladle, with which he scoops water and washes each hand in turn before replacing the ladle. To give an air of solidity, it is best if the *tsukubai* looks sunken into the ground.

Between the first stone and the

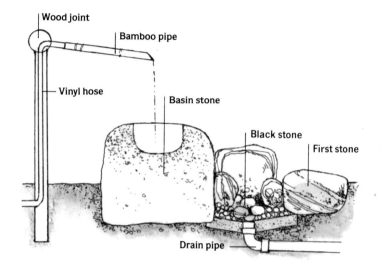

tsukubai is a small rocky hollow, which should be made impermeable and equipped with a drain. The water should never lie still in it and it should be continually cleared of leaves. Both drain and base should be covered with small, round, black stones, which will gleam when splashed with water from the main vessel.

Though there are few examples now, a large urn used to be placed under the drain to catch the water. The sound of a drop splashing on the water within the urn was amplified, so that even though it came from deep below the earth, it sounded uncannily close at hand.

Water is fed into the *tsukubai* through a length of bamboo, which is attached to a garden hose. Make sure the hose is not visible, otherwise the rustic effect will be marred. Alternatively, water can be supplied from the base of the *tsukubai*, creating the effect of a spring. Take care to regulate the flow, so that it does not pour out too forcefully. Often the water is left running so that it looks as if it is emanating from a natural spring. This effect can be enhanced by planting around the bamboo.

The water will flow over the rim of the vessel at one point only, pouring into the rocky hollow at its base. After several years, mosses will begin to grow on the rock, which will add interest to the water feature. Alternatively, you can place the *tsukubai* in the centre of a larger rocky hollow, in which case the water should be made to flow over all sides evenly.

The hollow should be about 6 inches (15cm) deep, and perhaps 16 inches (40cm) in diameter. Using the waterproofing technique discussed above, line the hollow with butyl or cement. Large stones should be placed around the edge and small stones should cover the base. The drain catching the water.

Since the *tsukubai* will probably not be functional outside Japan, elsewhere it must be used in the garden for visual and sound effect. Illumination at night, for example, often works very well.

The *tsukubai* is not difficult to construct, but, as with most water features, a great deal depends on the personal aspirations of the garden designer. Having chosen the vessel, embed it in the earth, so that 8 - 12in (20 - 30cm) remain above ground. Use a spirit level to determine the ideal surface-level of the water, so that it falls down over the chosen side of the vessel. At the same time, you should always try to make the rim appear as level as possible.

The simple outward appearance of a *tsukubai* belies the subtlety and ritual significance of its design.

WHAT TYPE OF WATER FEATURE?

Choose a water feature to reflect the way you feel about your garden. A single-jet fountain, for example, can display a simple elegance that recalls the Islamic tradition of water gardening. A formal pool, on the other hand, can utilize any number of interestiung shapes and patterns; while a Japanese-style garden is easy to create, with the help of some cobble-stones, rocks and a simple bridge.

There is scope for a water feature in almost every type and style of garden, as we have shown in the preceding pages. Assess the particular style of your garden and the space you have available, as well as the feeling you wish to evoke, by referring to them. Then choose whatever type of water feature fits your plan best.

If you choose an Islamic style, for example, remember that it is based on a deep respect for water, and rarely features plants. The shape should be well-defined and formal, and the treatment of water almost abstract. Typically, small Islamic water features include the use of an elegant round

basin with a simple fountain, or a millstone on which water forms a thin film. On a larger scale, try creating a pool that resembles the brimming courtyard pool of an Islamic mosque — perhaps softening the design by the restrained use of plants.

A Japanese-style water feature will offer a refined contemplative touch to your garden, and is ideal for a town garden because it can be realized on a small scale. One of the most interesting small features of such gardens is a *tsukubai*, or water basin. As in an Islamic water garden, the structure and beauty of a Japanese garden will depend on inorganic shapes, such as those of rocks.

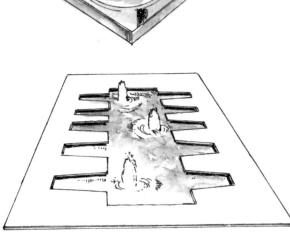

Be sure to introduce a variety of interesting plants into a natural garden.

With surprisingly little water, for example, the effect of a stream can be created by using cobbles for the river bed and rocks to indicate its course. Give the design an idea of movement and space by building a simple stone bridge, and remember to use appropriate accessories: a stone lantern, or perhaps a bamboo fence.

By contrast, an informal water garden can express a love of plants and an intimacy with nature. Informal styles provide great scope for the use of rockeries and waterfalls, but require more space and light than preceding styles. This is because their attraction relies on abstractions, such as the beauty of plants and on the shapes of pools. So consider the surroundings carefully before you decide to build this type of water feature. For example, an informal pool will look strange next to modern architecture unless you make an effort to blend one into the other.

Formal water features can be great fun, because they can incorporate a fountain. There is an enormous choice of designs: large or small, ornamental or plain. So before you start to design a formal water feature, decide whether you want to express dignity and elegance or effervescence and vitality.

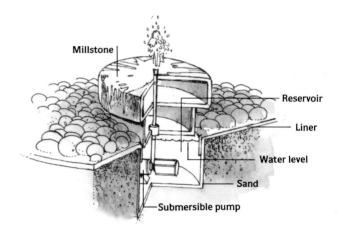

Millstone — Reservoir — Liner — Water level — Sand — Submersible pump

A mill-stone echoes some of the restraint of Islamic garden design when turned into a water feature. Tub gardens are ideal for gardens where space is limited. They are easy to make from barrels or stone basins.

LIGHTING

A light can be an interesting design-feature during the daytime as well as at night.

A sunken light can be made to swivel on an axis.

One mistake, made all too frequently, is to treat lighting as an accessory, when it should be an integral part of any garden design. Think carefully before you position your lights, considering how best you can make the most of your garden's potential during daytime and night-time. However attractive your garden is during the day, effective lighting can help to create a completely different kind of beauty and atmosphere after darkness falls.

Lighting can alter the way a garden is perceived, enhancing already attractive forms and shapes, and disguising less appealing features. In a town garden, for example, you could try to shade out the neighbouring houses. With a little thought, other intrinsic weaknesses in a garden can be turned to advantage in a similar way; with planning, they can even be made to take on a positively romantic allure.

A number of different styles of light are on the market. If you choose carefully, you will find that, far from looking clumsy and out of place during the day, a sequence of lights, thoughtfully placed, makes an interesting design feature and one that contrasts well with the natural environment.

But when a sequence of lights is to be used, try to stick to one common type or shape. This will give the scheme a sense of unity. Be careful, though, that you do not overdo the lighting. Like any component in the garden, lighting should not be used frivolously: each light should either focus on a specific feature

or illuminate an obstacle that might otherwise be difficult to negotiate — steps, or a pathway, for example.

Ornamental lighting can be used in a variety of ways. Try directing a light into the trees, to create a wonderful dappled effect; or experiment by covering your lights with perforated shapes.

Make the most of the effect of light on water, by illuminating waterfalls and fountains. If a light is placed so that it shines from below the water surface (take care, because special, heavily insulated fittings are needed for this) it will be captured within the water, forming a dramatic white plume or sheet against a dark background. In still water, this arrangement can be used to make a feature of the submarine world of aquatic plants and fish.

An illuminated jet is created by placing the light directly under the fountain.

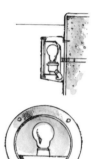

Remember that underwater lights will require special, heavily insulated fittings.

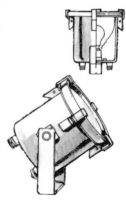

Spotlights can be used to draw attention to the most attractive features in the garden.

FISH

The vivid colour and movement of fish add another rich dimension to the pool, embuing its placid surface with life and lending mystery to its hidden depths. One of the results of looking after fish, will be a healthy pool environment. Fish control aquatic insect life, which damages leaves; they also eat the larvae of annoying mosquitoes.

Fish do not, in fact, need much care and attention. Their requirements are sufficient food, plant protection, and well-oxygenated water. Care must be taken that the water is not polluted by dissolved metal ions, which might react if the piping is new, and also that there is no chance of weedkiller poisoning the pool. Cement can also harm fish if it is not treated with *Silglaze*.

It is important not to over-stock the pool, as this will result in a lack of oxygen and also a build-up of poison through waste excretion. For this reason, it is recommended that for every square foot (0.093 metres square) of water, 2 inches (6 centimetres) of fish is acceptable.

It is best to wait a month before stocking the pool to allow the water to establish ecological stability and to give the oxygenating plants a chance to root. (*See Planting and Maintenance*). You should introduce the fish in two stages, to see how they adapt to pool-conditions.

When choosing fish, look out for healthy specimens. Select active fish with erect dorsal fins. Do not choose fish with rotted fins. White spots indicate a fungal disease, which might be a result of damage, and although not contagious, afflicted fish should be avoided.

The most popular varieties of fish include the Goldfish, Shubunkin, Comet and Golden Orfe. Unlike the other three, the Orfe is not a variety of Goldfish. It is an excellent pond-fish, providing lively surface entertainment as well as snapping up insect life.

Fish food comes in either pellets or flakes. Pellets are preferable as they float, attracting the fish up to the surface of the water. If feeding takes place at a regular hour, the fish soon become tame and will gather at the pool-side. The quantity of food depends on the time of year, and it is advisable to consult your supplier. Generally speaking, however, fish will require feeding three times a day during the summer, slightly more frequently during the autumn, and more often again in winter.

Fish will need protection from the sun on hot days, and this can be provided by lilies. Oxygenators are also useful to protect eggs, which can be laid in the foliage. For this reason, you should wait before trimming the plants, until the eggs have hatched.

All sorts of aquatic life add interest to the pool and help maintain a healthy ecological environment.

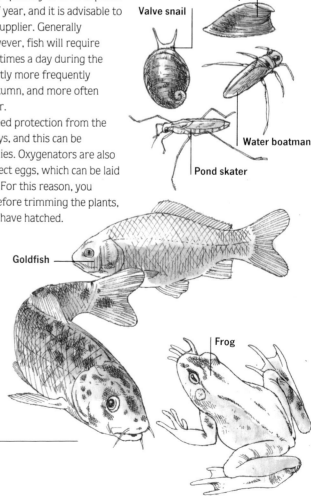

PLANTING AND MAINTENANCE

Plant water lilies in perforated containers, to ensure maximum health and easy maintenance.

Marginals and oxygenators, too, can be planted in containers, by the water and in it, to give a splash of colour and life to a water feature.

It is more convenient to plant aquatic plants and marginals in containers, than to fill the entire pool with soil, as this causes maintenance problems. The more voracious plants will start taking over the pool and it is an unpleasant job trying to extricate and divide them. Disturbing the pool floor will also sully the water. It is therefore best to plant in movable containers, which are fixed with earth and raised on bricks to the suitable planting depth, (*see plant index*). This method is a much more convenient means of maintainance, since the containers are easily accessible, making plant division and earth changing — which should be carried out every few years — a simple procedure.

The best kind of container is a wide and shallow plastic vessel, perforated to allow movement of water. Cement containers are difficult to move and should not be used unless treated with *Silglaze*. The container should be filled with a loamy soil mixture, as used in the bog garden. You can add a small amount of seasoned fertilizer or bonemeal to

this mixture, but take care not to pollute the water with the wrong kind of fertilizer, as this will sour the water and might also affect the food chain.

LILIES

Like all aquatic plants, lilies should be planted when the water has warmed up a bit, so the correct time will vary according to climate. The growing point or "nose" should protrude slightly from the soil, and then the remaining soil surface should be covered with a layer of gravel. This anchors the plants and prevents them from being disturbed by fish. The container should be thoroughly soaked before being sunk into the water to prevent air bubbles from disrupting the soil and muddying the water.

MARGINALS

Marginals can be planted in the same way as lilies. It is a good idea to plant each marginal in a separate container, in order to protect weaker plants from competition from stronger ones.

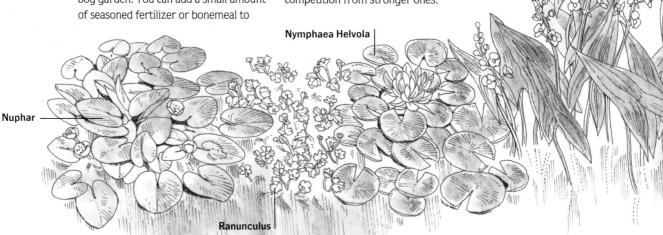

Nuphar

Nymphaea Helvola

Ranunculus

Iris

Sagittaria

OXYGENATORS

Oxygenators are easy to plant, as their roots do not need to be embedded in the soil. Place them in containers and weigh them down, using a strip of lead or wire so that they do not float about. Be careful not to leave them to long in the sun, out of water, as they will dry up quickly.

MAINTENANCE

A pool is not difficult to maintain, provided an ecological balance is established. This takes about a month. As water in most newly filled pools is alkaline, chemical changes will turn the water cloudy. Then, as algae thrives in alkaline conditions, the water will turn green. As the aquatic plants mature, the water will become acid and the algae coloration will diminish until the water becomes clear.

As mentioned above, it will be necessary to divide the water lilies and thin the oxygenators, in order to prevent them becoming too invasive. The latter may be broken up by hand, but preferably use a pair of scissors. Cut away about a third of the plant, taking care to leave the healthiest looking areas. Water lilies should be divided, every three or four years, when there is too much leaf growth and too few flowers. You should divide the lilies in late spring by slicing through the tuber.

Orontium aquaticum

The divided rootstock, or rhizome, can be replanted, but first the thick and hairless anchor roots can be cut off, as they serve no purpose. Nutrition is absorbed through the slender roots which have small black roothairs.

You should also divide marginal plants. To do this, you simply prise the root apart, using a small handfork.

In autumn, the horticulturalist's water feature will begin to look sad. The leaves and stems will turn brown and sag in the water. The best thing to do is to clear the pond of dead foliage and dredge out the fallen leaves, which will otherwise decompose in the water, releasing noxious gases and causing considerable discomfort to fish.

If there are trees near the pool, it is best to lay some netting over it. This will also discourage predators, such as herons or gulls. The dead leaves and stalks of the marginal plants should be cut back and burnt.

In the winter months, icing over can be a problem. The expansion and contraction of ice will crack cement pools. To prevent this, place a piece of wood or a soft ball on the surface of the water. Fish will also suffer if the surface is completely iced over, and you need to make a hole to allow them to breathe. This is a simple process of pouring boiling water over an area of the ice.

Excessive cold will not harm the plant life, as long as it is covered by at least nine inches (23 cm) of water. Tropical water lilies might need winter protection, in which case they should be lifted, drained and protected with moss, leaves and branches. Other plants, which cannot winter outside, should be lifted and kept in water in a cool place until springtime.

Bulrushes can make a striking feature in a water garden. Sometimes growing higher than a person, they flower in July and August, growing characteristic cylindrical reddish-brown spikelets.

SELECTIVE PLANT LIST

There is an enormous variety of water lilies. When choosing water lilies for your pool, there are a few basic rules to follow. Firstly, much will depend on its size; water lilies with large spreads will choke a small pool. As you should hope to cover between a half and two thirds of the water surface, a 50ft square pool will need about 30ft square of plant cover, (a four metre square pool should have approximately two and a half metres square cover). This area can then be allocated plants from groups A to F, below. The lilies should be chosen for the colour and shape and shape of their leaves as well as their flowers. Remember that sun is a prerequisite for optimum flowering. Hardy water lilies require four hours of direct sunlight a day, while tropical water lilies need five to six.

The following list is categorized according to planting depth and size of spread. Note that the planting depth refers to the distance from the water level to the earth level.

	GROUP NAME	SIZE OF PLANT	DESCRIPTION
	The prefix N refers to the generic name Nymphaea		
A	N. Pygmaea alba	3-9 inch depth (approx. 8-23 cm) 1.5 foot spread (approx. 45 cm)	Tiny one-inch white flower. Seed germinates freely.
	N. Pygmaea helvola	3-9 inch depth (approx. 8-23 cm) 1.5 foot spread (approx. 45 cm)	Canary yellow flower with olive green leaves mottled with reddish brown dots.
	N. Pygmaea rubra	3-9 inch depth (approx. 8-23 cm) 1.5 foot spread (approx. 45 cm)	Blood red flower with purplish green foliage larger than either alba or helvola.
	N. Mexicana	3-9 inch depth (approx. 8-23 cm) 1.5 foot spread (approx. 45 cm)	Yellow flower with purple mottled leaves and a reddish underside. It stands several inches above the ground.
B	Laydkeri lilalea	5-12 inch depth (approx. 13-30 cm) 2 foot spread (approx. 60 cm)	Pink flower.
	Aurora	5-12 inch depth (approx. 13-30 cm) 2 foot spread (approx. 60 cm)	Yellow flower which matures into orange and finally dark red.

GROUP NAME	SIZE OF PLANT	DESCRIPTION
C **N. Laydekeri fulgens**	7-15 inch depth (approx. 18-38 cm) 3 foot spread (approx. 90 cm)	Crimson flowers with reddish centres.
N. Froebeli	7-15 inch depth (approx. 18-38 cm) 3 foot spread (approx. 90 cm)	Similar to fulgens but flowers have an orange centre.
N. Laydekeri purpurata	7-15 inch depth (approx. 18-38 cm) 3 foot spread (approx. 90 cm)	Deep crimson purple with orange centre and whitish tints on the petals.
N. Graziella	7-15 inch depth (approx. 18-38 cm) 3 foot spread (approx. 90 cm)	Orange blossoms.
N. Hermine	7-15 inch depth (approx. 18-38 cm) 3 foot spread (approx. 90 cm)	Pure white star-shaped flowers with beautiful leaves.
D **N. James brydon**	9-18 inch depth (approx. 23-46 cm) 4 foot spread (approx. 120 cm)	Rose pink flowers with deep orange centres and dark circular leaves. Will tolerate a little shade.
N. Albatross	9-18 inch depth (approx. 23-46 cm) 4 foot spread (approx. 120 cm)	Large white flowers with purple leaves maturing to a bright green.
N. Rose arey	9-18 inch depth (approx. 23-46 cm) 4 foot spread (approx. 120 cm)	Long pointed pink petals.
E **N. William falconer**	9-24 inch depth (approx. 23-60 cm) 5 foot spread (approx. 150 cm)	Crimson red flowers with dark handsome leaves.
N. Gonnêre (also known as snowball)	9-24 inch depth (approx. 23-60 cm) 5 foot spread (approx. 150 cm)	Large pure white 5-6 inch (13-15 cm) dense flowers.
N. Paul hariot	9-24 inch depth (approx. 23-60 cm) 5 foot spread (approx. 150 cm)	Apricot yellow flowers change to orange pink before deepening to red. Maroon mottled foliage.
F **N. Conqueror**	12-30 inch depth (approx. 30-75 cm) 6 foot spread (approx. 180 cm)	Crimson blossoms that flower profusely.
N. Amabilis (also known as pink maruel)	12-30 inch depth (approx. 30-75 cm) 6 foot spread (approx. 180 cm)	Salmon pink flowers mature into a rose pink.
N. Marlialea chromatella	12-30 inch depth (approx. 30-75 cm) 6 foot spread (approx. 180 cm)	6-7 inch (15-18 cm) soft yellow flowers which open later in the day. It will tolerate shade.
N. Escarboucle	9-24 inch depth (approx. 23-60 cm) 5 foot spread (approx. 150 cm)	Large bright crimson blooms, yellow tipped with reddish stamens.

Other surface plants		
Nymphoides peltata		3 inch (7.6 cm) bright green mottled leaves with dainty yellow flowers standing a few inches above water. As it is invasive, it ought to be ruthlessly pruned.

NAME	SIZE OF PLANT	DESCRIPTION
Nuphars		The leaf shape similar to **nymphaea.** Except for **nuphar pumila**, not suitable for pools. Has the advantage of growing in moving water. Inconspicuous yellow flowers from June to August and oval leaves.
Adonegeton distachyus		Water hawthorn, best alternative to water lily tolerating moderate shade. White-lobed flowers with a black stamens have strong vanilla scent and flower even during mild winters. Oblong leaves. Any depth.

OXYGENATING PLANTS

The submerged oxygenating plants are integral to pool life creating clear algae-free water. Without them, microscopic life would soon saturate the pond water turning it green. Oxygenating plants, a more evolved form of life, efficiently extract the mineral salts from the water, depriving algae of nutrients. At the same time they provide necessary shelter, food and oxygen for fish. A pool under 100 ft square will require a bunch for every two foot square. (A pool 10 metres square will need a bunch for every one third of a square metre.) If the pool size is over 100 foot square it will require less. Oxygenators should never exceed one third of the pool's surface area. Though generally forming a carpet, some do have visible flowers. The most popular forms include:

NAME	SIZE OF PLANT	DESCRIPTION
Elodea canadensis (Canadian pondweed)		– a free-floating dark green dense carpet which is easily cropped by hand. It produces tiny flowers from May to October, which according to a South African cookery book, can be used to flavour meat dishes.
Hottonia palustris		– Water violet with 8-16 inch (20-40 cm) spikes of pale mauve flowers from May to August. Light green feathery foliage. It requires partial shade and prefers soft water and acid soil.
Ranunculus aquatilis		– mass of one inch white flowers with gold centres from May to August. Dark green foliage.
Ceratophyllum demersum (hornwort)		Non-rooted dark green feathery foliage on brittle stems which is easily controlled. It requires sun and depth.
Lobelia dortmanna (water Lobelia)		An evergreen, entirely submerged plant with long thin leaves and small light blue flowers.

NAME	SIZE OF PLANT	DESCRIPTION
Calla palustris (bog arum)	Height 6 inches (approx. 15cm) P.D 2-6 inches (approx. 5-15cm)	– Ground-covering spreader with glosy leaves and white sheath-like flowers in May or June. Red berries herald the autumn. Requires a lime-free soil.
Catha palustris (mark marigold)	Height 1-2½ feet (approx. 30-75cm) Shallow water and? mud	– Large golden flowers from March to July with attractive round, veined leaves.
Iris kaemferi (Japanese iris)	Height 36 inches (approx. 90cm)	– Exotic plant with a variety of subtle colours. Prefers water in the growing season but not in winter. Alkaline soil is fatal.
Iris laevigata (water iris)	Height 2 feet (approx. 60cm) P.D 2-5 inches (approx. 20-30cm)	– Lavender blue flowers in early summer. White, pink, yellow cultivars have been produced.
Orontium aquaticum (golden club)	Height 10 inches (approx. 25cm) P.D 6-12 inches (approx. 15-30cm)	– Orchid-like mottled yellow flowers from July onwards.
Pontederia cordata (pickerel)	Height 20 inches (approx. 50cm) P.D 6-12 inches (approx. 15-30cm)	– Blue flower spikes in the late summer and big clumps of spear-shaped waxy green leaves on long stalks.
Sagittaria sagittifolia (common arrowhead	Height 2-3 feet (approx. 60-90cm) P.D 4-6 inches (approx. 10-15cm)	– White flowers with purple centres and distinctive three-pointed leaves – hence "arrowhead". Flowers in July and August.
Scirpus zebrina (zebra rush)	Height 3-4 ft (approx. 90-120cm) P.D 6-12 inches (approx. 15-30cm)	– Distinctive green and white striped leaves. Occasional plain green stems should be cut out.
Typha minima (reed mace)	Height 1½ feet (approx. 46cm) P.D 3-6 inches (approx. 8-15cm)	– Shortest of the typha family. With bluish green spiky leaves and brown pokers.

Waterside plants

Marginal plants will be planted outside the water limit. Common yet striking plants in this category include Astilbes, Hostas, Primulas and Irises.

Astilbe and **Arendsii**	Height 2-3 feet (approx. 60-90cm)	– Refers to a group of cultivars with richly coloured plumes and delicate foliage. Flowers from June into August.
Hosta	Height 20 inches (approx. 50cm)	– Bold luxuriant foliage plants which will not tolerate excesssive sun. flowers in the summer. Their leaves are susceptible to slugs.
Primulas	Varying height	– Drumstick or candelabra species with flowers appearing in tiers. Colours vary greatly. Flower in the summer. These plants prefer acid soil.
Iris sibirica	Height 3 feet (approx. 90cm)	– Many varieties of blue, purple and white flowers forming dense clumps of grassy foliage. Flowers in the summer. Though a waterside plant, it will adapt to drier conditions.

INDEX

ACKNOWLEDGEMENTS

Morgan Samuel Editions would like to thank the following persons and organizations, to whom copyright in the photographs noted belongs:

Cover Clive Boursnell
8 Clive Boursnell; **11** Clive Boursnell; **13** Clive Boursnell; **15** Clive Boursnell; **17** Clive Boursnell; **19** Clive Boursnell; **21** Clive Boursnell; **23** Tatsui Takenosuke; **25** Tatsui Takenosuke; **27** Clive Boursnell; **29** Clive Boursnell; **31** Clive Boursnell

The author wishes to thank Masaru and Naoko Isobe, Tatsui Takenosuke, Ken Nakajima, the Royal Institute of British Architects, the Royal Horticultural Society and Derek Lovejoy & Partners for their invaluable help.